FIELDCRAFT AND STEALTH

FIELDCRAFT *and* STEALTH

THE TRAINING OF THE SOLDIER IN
STALKING—CRAWLING—
PATROLLING

By

LT.-COL. N. A. D. ARMSTRONG
O.B.E., R.M.

Commandant The Royal Marine Snipers' School

*Late Chief Reconnaissance Officer, Canadian Army
Chief Instructor, 2nd Army School of Scouting,
Observation and Sniping, Flanders, 1915-16*

*Commandant, Canadian Corps School of Scouting,
Observation and Sniping, France, 1917-18*

*Late Senior Instructor, Sniping Wing, Small Arms
School, Hythe and Bisley, 1940-42*

Author of
" Fieldcraft, Sniping and Intelligence "
" After Big Game in The Upper Yukon "
etc.

The Naval & Military Press Ltd

Published by

The Naval & Military Press Ltd

Unit 5 Riverside, Brambleside
Bellbrook Industrial Estate
Uckfield, East Sussex
TN22 1QQ England

Tel: +44 (0)1825 749494

www.naval-military-press.com
www.nmarchive.com

CONTENTS

FIELDCRAFT AND STEALTH

TRAINING

FIELDCRAFT—STALKING—CRAWLING AND STEALTH METHODS

Method of conducting a Practical Demonstration with Commentary.

MEN.—Four to six. If possible, about the same height (5 ft. 8 in. or thereabouts) ; build not too heavy (about 11 stone).

EQUIPMENT.—Rifles ; pistols ; grenades (dummies) ; woollen caps ; camouflage nets from helmets ; gloves (leather or woollen) ; gym. shoes or rubber ankle boots, or, failing either of these, then the black service boot.

SOUND.—If the demonstration is to be given to a large number of soldiers—250 or more—then it is desirable to obtain a Public Address Unit (microphone) so that all may hear the commentary.

LAYOUT.—It is important to note position of sun when arranging the demonstration. The most convenient position for all concerned is for the sun to be on a flank. If this cannot be obtained, then the sun must be behind the spectators.

DIAGRAM 1.—Suggested position of spectators, conducting officer and demonstration squad.

7

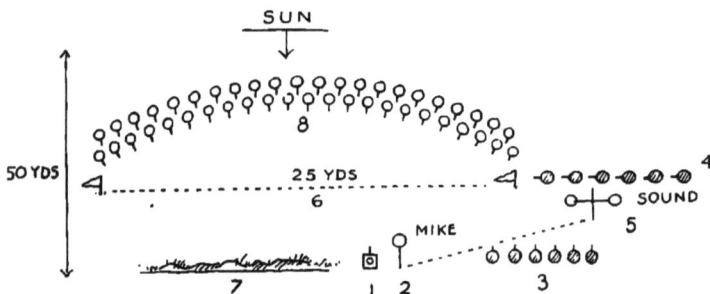

DIAGRAM I.

1. Conducting officer.

2. Microphone, slightly to a flank.

3. Position of scouts standing at ease with rifles grounded during opening remarks (ten minutes).

4. Position of scouts after opening talk in readiness to commence demonstration—single file. Either four or six scouts can be used.

5. Sound megaphones. Out to a flank to avoid obstructing view of conducting officer. Direction of a strong wind must be noted and megaphones adjusted accordingly.

6. Demonstration area. Flags about twenty-five yards apart. Scouts demonstrate each movement between these flags.

7. Position of any equipment such as camouflage for scouts or snipers, or any " gadgets " which the conducting officer wishes to display to the spectators during the period allowed for his talk and demonstration on camouflage.

8. Spectators arranged in a semicircle with each flank close to a flag as per Diagram I.

Note.—This is the layout as practised successfully by the author, and is produced here only as a suggestion which can be altered to suit any individual instructor.

8

LOCATION.—If it is desired to include in the demonstration a practical display of individual camouflage as well as a final demonstration of Scout *v*. Scout, then it will be necessary to find some ground where cover—such as long grass, small shrubs, weeds, rough ground—exists ; also trees (either large or small), bushes, etc.

If it is desired to demonstrate Fieldcraft only, then any small field with level surface will be sufficient.

Note.—It is important to ascertain if all spectators can see and hear both demonstration and commentary.

PLATOON TRAINING.

⟐ PLATOON COMMANDER
↓

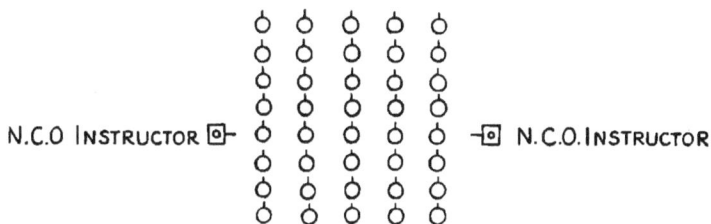

N.C.O INSTRUCTOR ⊡⊢   ○ ○ ○ ○ ○   ⊣⊡ N.C.O. INSTRUCTOR
                      ○ ○ ○ ○ ○
                      ○ ○ ○ ○ ○
                      ○ ○ ○ ○ ○
                      ○ ○ ○ ○ ○
                      ○ ○ ○ ○ ○
                      ○ ○ ○ ○ ○
                      ○ ○ ○ ○ ○

DIAGRAM 2.

9

OPENING TALK

Fieldcraft.

Fieldcraft is an art, but not a new art. It has been practised for centuries, but, even so, the fundamental principles remain the same to-day although they may be applied differently under certain conditions of warfare.

For instance, Fieldcraft as practised by the so-called Red Indians of North America for generations remains the same to-day in many respects ; we cannot teach them very much where stealth is concerned.

Historical References to Fieldcraft.

It has been stated that there is scarcely a battle in history that has not been lost or won in proportion to the value of the previous reconnaissance.

The great Duke of Marlborough was a good scout himself and was much impressed with the value of fieldcraft.

Much of Oliver Cromwell's success was traceable to the information he received through his " scout masters," who were highly trained in fieldcraft.

Practical Training.

To-day we are told that training in the use of ground should begin at the outset of the soldier's service. It must be remembered that a large proportion of the men in our new armies have spent their lives in towns and are therefore accustomed to flat surfaces and restricted field of vision, and to streets brilliantly lit at night. Therefore their instinct for use of ground and darkness will be lacking.

Like all work of an intensely practical nature, the best and only way to teach fieldcraft is by demonstration, imitation, practice and experience. It cannot be taught in the lecture-room.

Definition of Fieldcraft.

Fieldcraft is the art of the hunter, coupled with the wiles of the poacher. This includes concealment, silent movement, knowledge of his prey, and skill with his weapon; also the use of both natural cover and camouflage in conjunction with movement.

In peace time the hunter has to outwit his quarry. The quarry may have powers of evasion—quickness of eye, sense of smell, speed of movement—but as a rule he has small power of retaliation.

In war the sniper or scout has to outwit his fellow-man; cunning is opposed to cunning, and each side has full power of retaliation—the sniper if he fails may lose his life.

Unlimited patience is essential. No two stalks or stealth patrols or reconnaissance patrols are ever likely to be the same. The objective may be close; it may be many miles away. It may take minutes or it may take hours.

It may be necessary to stalk over many different types of ground and cover.

No expert scout can tell you in so many words *how* he carries out his stalk; he moves instinctively from knowledge gained by much experience.

To become an expert in fieldcraft one's brain must be constantly active and on the alert—thinking ahead, so to speak: taking advantage of ground and cover, light and shade, wind, noise, rain, mist, snow—ever on the alert.

It also creates initiative and self-reliance.

Another advantage is that recruits are keenly interested in fieldcraft as opposed to barrack-square training.

In scouting as in all games of skill, footwork and balance is of vital importance; also keen observation and concentration, perfect physical condition with supple and agile limbs.

Finally, it should be stressed that the particular object of the demonstration about to be given is for the purpose of training recruits in fieldcraft in a simple and elementary way and maintaining a correct and progressive sequence until proficiency is gained.

In giving instruction in these methods to small squads of men say up to platoon strength, it will not be necessary to arrange for microphone installation; one or more trained instructors can be used for demonstrating each movement, after which sections can assemble in single file laterally and in line and proceed to imitate the movements demonstrated by the instructors.

The foregoing concludes the opening talk.

DEMONSTRATION COMMENCES

The instructor reminds spectators that all drill or barrack-square movements are eliminated and stealth used in its place. He will also state about how many hours of individual training his squad has had.

It is desirable to demonstrate that, if instructors will follow the author's sequence of training as illustrated in this book, any recruit of average intelligence can perform all the movements with not more than twelve hours' intensive training over a period of one week.

Then the instructor, addresses the demonstration squad, orders them to take station in single file behind red flag on right flank (see Diagram 1). He then tells them :—

" You are a reconnaissance patrol leaving your headquarters in the battle zone. It is night and seeing distance is some thirty yards. You are out to obtain information and re-establish touch with the enemy. Speed is essential. You must not fight if such can be avoided. The question of equipment will be dealt with later on."

Note.—It is advisable to impress the above instructions on the minds of young recruits, otherwise their brains concentrate on mundane affairs and they fail to take note of the work they are doing or trying to do.

The instructor orders scouts to carry on ; he calls for each movement in the following sequence

RIGHT METHOD WITHOUT ARMS

WALKING (STOOPING) : RIGHT METHOD.

Head and shoulders carried in a slightly stooping position helps to break outline.

Enemy probably not in very close proximity ; not considered necessary to crawl.

Speed essential compatible with safety.

Arms and hands held loosely but close to body ; feet raised sufficiently to clear surface of ground.   Toes and ball of feet down first, followed by heel.

Walk stealthily, watching all round carefully.

Scouts all conform to movements of leader.

WRONG METHOD WITHOUT ARMS

WALKING (STOOPING): WRONG METHOD.

Leading scout walks out between flags, swinging arms and hands.

Head erect and moved jerkily.

Heels down first instead of toes.

General appearance of stealth is lacking.

WALKING (CROUCHING) : RIGHT METHOD.

Getting closer to the enemy, but leader considers it unnecessary to crawl.

Bend the knees as much as possible without touching the ground ; arms slightly extended to give balance ; hands ready to take weight of body to deaden sound of fall ; feet raised slightly and turned slightly outwards.

Watch flanks carefully and watch all round.

Stealthy movement of head ; head in line with shoulders.

Leader when half-way between flags should come down stealthily on one knee and watch and listen for a minute ; scouts conform ; move back into position very stealthily and forward again.

16

WRONG METHOD WITHOUT ARMS

WALKING (CROUCHING) : WRONG METHOD.

Walking forward with back bent and an exaggerated " stoop."

Head downwards and eyes concentrated on the ground.

No alertness visible.

Arms and hands moving with each step.

CRAWLING ON HANDS AND KNEES : RIGHT METHOD.

Closer to enemy, but not yet necessary to crawl on stomach.

No quick or sudden movements of hands, body or feet ; take long reach with each knee.

Knees should if possible occupy the position just vacated by each hand.

Raise each foot to clear the surface of the ground.

Head in line with shoulders, kept low.

Watch flanks frequently—stop—look—listen.

Japs in all their fighting make continual use of crawling in this method in conjunction with camouflage, both artificial and natural.

CRAWLING ON HANDS AND KNEES : WRONG METHOD.

Many mistakes are perpetrated in this position which would require many photographs to illustrate.

The photograph above illustrates perhaps the most dangerous error in this movement :

Elbows bent and touching the ground.

Scout's " posterior " assuming the appearance of a small mountain in the air—like the " invisible " ostrich with his head buried in the sand.

CRAWLING ON ELBOWS AND KNEES : RIGHT METHOD.

Called " The Roll." Closer to the ground than last movement ; more difficult to spot by enemy.

Turn slowly and stealthily from side to side, propelled by each knee and forearm in turn ; head close to ground. Watch flanks.

Faster than crawling on stomach. Nearer to enemy.

WRONG METHOD WITHOUT ARMS

CRAWLING ON ELBOWS AND KNEES : WRONG METHOD.

The main error in this movement is to raise the head and feet in the air and to lift the body from the ground when changing from one knee to the other ; also in keeping the hands and wrists locked under the chest as illustrated in crawling on the stomach.

CRAWLING ON STOMACH : RIGHT METHOD.

Difficult, and important to practise. Must be physically fit in every way. Used by patrols both by day and night; move inches at a time; possibly may be out for several hours. Lie flat on stomach, legs and feet together, heels down, face almost touching ground. Move forward by closing right hand on left wrist or *vice versa* and using forearms and elbows only. To look to the rear raise right or left elbow and look under armpit.

WRONG METHOD WITHOUT ARMS

CRAWLING ON STOMACH : WRONG METHOD.

Legs wide apart.   Toes in ground and heels in the air.

Head raised and elbows carried too far back at the end of the forward movement.

RIGHT METHOD WITHOUT ARMS

MOVE SIDEWAYS—MOVING TO A FLANK : RIGHT METHOD.

It is necessary to change direction of advance sometimes to obtain new cover without being seen, etc.

Keep flat on stomach, legs together, and facing your front.

Move whole body on ground.

Do not lift stomach from ground.

Move slowly to a flank.

WRONG METHOD WITHOUT ARMS

MOVE SIDEWAYS—MOVING TO A FLANK : WRONG METHOD.

Reaching out with one leg.

Body twisted into an oblique position to the line of advance, and raising the body from the ground.

Head raised ; heels in the air.

MOVE BACKWARDS : RIGHT METHOD.

Same as forward : feet together.

Use forearms and elbows, keep body on the ground.

This is an important movement for scouts to know; often used to back out of sudden dangerous position developing.

26

WRONG METHOD WITHOUT ARMS

MOVE BACKWARDS : WRONG METHOD.

Legs apart ; heels in the air ; head raised, also shoulders.

RIGHT METHOD WITHOUT ARMS

Turning Round : Right Method.

RIGHT METHOD

An important movement for all scouts to know and practise, particularly when on night reconnaissance or on stealth patrol. Lie flat on stomach, face close to the ground, legs together. To turn completely round to the right with the least possible noise and visibility, first of all reach out as far as possible with the left leg, then turn the upper part of the body round to the right; then close up the right foot to the left and repeat the movement. With practice this movement can be completed in a few minutes.

WRONG METHOD WITHOUT ARMS

TURNING ROUND : WRONG METHOD.

By a combination of nearly all the errors mentioned in the foregoing movements. Worst error is to raise the body on hands and knees and turn round.

CROSSING A ROAD : RIGHT METHOD.

A noiseless method of crossing a road.
The leading scout crawls up on hands and knees to roadside ;
makes careful visual reconnaissance up and down and across
road—looks for any shadows, trees, houses, etc.
Cross in shadows if possible or at a sharp bend in the road.
Cross in pairs or threes close together *in line*, not single file.
Use hands and knees and raise feet from road and retain them
in that position ; quite noiseless.   Useful if crawling on gravel.

WRONG METHOD WITHOUT ARMS

CROSSING A ROAD : WRONG METHOD.

Common error, crossing in single file at intervals at the double.

Arms and hands swinging " fore and aft."

Or walking across in stooping position without any degree of stealth.

WRONG METHODS WITHOUT ARMS

Wrong Methods.

If it is desired to " lay on " a special demonstration for a selected audience, it will be found necessary to modify some of the movements in order to save time, and it is suggested that nearly all the " wrong " methods can be concentrated into one movement as follows :—

Patrol stands carelessly in the open under observation by enemy, discussing next movement and pointing in various directions—a common error by all reconnaissance parties.

Leading scout rushes forward.

Throws himself violently on ground, then raises himself quickly on knees.

Looks round with head well in the air and then waves vigorously for the remainder of patrol to join him.

Again more rushing and movement of feet in air.

Then each scout will carry on, making obvious errors ; face close to the ground with backside well in the air ; quick rushes on hands and knees ; then stop and look around with jerky movements of head, etc.

This movement concludes the first part of the demonstration.

The second part demonstrates the correct method of carrying a rifle by snipers or scouts, more particularly snipers by day ; rifle with or without telescopic sight.

WRONG METHODS WITHOUT ARMS.

How to carry a Rifle when Sniping or on Patrol.

Note.—Instructor has arranged that the demonstration scouts collect their rifles ; fall in as per drill order, and senior scout inspects rifles ; safety precautions. Explain that this constitutes the only drill movement in the demonstration.

RIGHT METHOD OF STALKING WITH A RIFLE

BALANCE AND HOLD : RIGHT METHOD.

Scouts demonstrate first position : rifle in left hand, muzzle pointing to front in line with left eye, butt close to right side of body ; right arm hanging loosely near right side with hand and wrist over butt without holding it. Hold sling tight against rifle. Explain briefly the value of sniping and use of telescope sights ; also snipers should all be trained to use the sling as it steadies the hold wonderfully. When stalking the sling should not be allowed to hang loose or drag along the ground. Stress the point that the right arm must be held close to the side without grasping the small of the butt ; the right hand is loose—helps to preserve balance and remove obstructions carefully, etc.

WRONG METHOD OF STALKING WITH A RIFLE

BALANCE AND HOLD : WRONG METHOD.

The demonstration squad will now demonstrate the wrong method of holding the rifle, still standing in the same position.

By grasping the rifle at the small.

Muzzle pointing over or towards the left shoulder.

Right elbow bent and forming a definite angle.

Very plainly seen at long distances by keen observers using telescope or binoculars.

RIGHT METHOD OF STALKING WITH A RIFLE

WALKING (STOOPING) : RIGHT METHOD.

As without rifle when " walking (stooping)."

Rifle in left hand at point of balance ; muzzle upwards, pointing to front ; rifle across body, butt on right thigh. Sling held up.

Right arm and hand close to side with hand over rifle butt, but not necessarily touching.

Keep on the alert, watch all round. May be an enemy sniper on either flank.

Can come into an aiming position very quickly in any direction.

WRONG METHOD OF STALKING WITH A RIFLE

WALKING (STOOPING): WRONG METHOD.

Rifle pointing to the left and well below the shoulder; sling loose; right hand grasping small of butt.

Dangerous angle presented by bent elbow and light visible between arm and body. Awkward position when advancing through cover.

RIGHT METHOD OF STALKING WITH A RIFLE.

WALKING (CROUCHING) : RIGHT METHOD.

Same position as without rifle—same stealthy movements.

Rifle in same position as when " walking (stooping)."

Demonstrate coming into aim on one knee with much stealth, bringing rifle slowly and stealthily into the aim at a supposed enemy sniper.

Point out that the sniper has moved and demonstrate how the rifle must be lowered with as much stealth as in aiming.

WRONG METHOD OF STALKING WITH A RIFLE

WALKING (CROUCHING) : WRONG METHOD.

Rifle still pointing to the left and carried in front of the body ; sling loose and right hand grasping butt.

Again demonstrating dangerous angle presented by elbow and light. Quite impossible to advance noiselessly through cover with rifle in this position.

RIGHT METHOD OF STALKING WITH A RIFLE

On Hands and Knees (Crawling) : Right Method.

Rifle in left hand, muzzle pointing to front and upwards, toe of butt just touching the ground to help balance rifle and take some weight from left hand.

Sling held up.

Demonstrate coming into aim from this position.

Note that the rifle is carried outside the right leg.

WRONG METHOD OF STALKING WITH A RIFLE

On Hands and Knees (Crawling) : Wrong Method.

A very common error—to use the rifle as a walking-stick by holding it at or near the point of balance and dragging it along, entirely oblivious of mud and water so far as the well-being of the rifle is concerned.

Another wrong method is to hold it near the muzzle and drag it along the ground.

RIGHT METHOD OF STALKING WITH A RIFLE

On Elbows and Knees (Crawling) : Right Method.

Point out that it is now becoming difficult to protect rifle and sight from obstructions, more particularly a telescope sight.

Rifle must be held slightly below point of balance, knuckles downward, butt turned over flat and on the ground, trigger guard turned outwards.

This position enables the scout to crawl forward as without a rifle, using forearms and hands.

Butt will be *under* the right arm, breech and sight off the ground.

Watch muzzle carefully as there is much danger of muzzle becoming blocked with mud or snow, etc. This happened frequently during 1914-18 war on the Somme and at Passchendaele.

WRONG METHOD OF STALKING WITH A RIFLE

ON ELBOWS AND KNEES (CRAWLING): WRONG METHOD.

Dragging it along the ground with the right hand, or to hold it in front of the body and at right angles and both hands grasping the rifle.

ON STOMACH (CRAWLING) : RIGHT METHOD.

This is the most difficult position for the sniper or scout when stalking close to the enemy or for the sportsman when stalking big game. The great danger is the fouling of the muzzle.

In this position the fore-end of the rifle must be rested on the left wrist with forearm flat on ground and in line with the shoulder ; right hand, knuckles downward, holding small of butt well over to the right side, so that muzzle points forward and not at right angles to line of advance.

Head must be kept low.

This, as the result of many years' experience, has proved to be the best position under all conditions both in peace and war.

WRONG METHOD OF STALKING WITH A RIFLE

On Stomach (Crawling): Wrong Method.

Balancing the rifle on both forearms at right angles to the body or throwing the rifle forward a few feet and at right angles to the body and crawling up to it, and repeating the performance.

WRONG METHODS OF STALKING OR PATROL-LING WITH RIFLE

If it is desired to lay on a special demonstration for a selected audience it will be necessary to omit some of the movements to save time, and it will be advisable to dispense with nearly all the individual wrong methods and concentrate them into one demonstration as follows.

The demonstration squad will show how these movements should not be carried out—viz., snipers run forward with rifle at the trail, in single file ; throw themselves on ground ; get up carelessly and crawl forward on hands and knees, holding rifle at point of balance and dragging it along the ground. Others hold rifle near muzzle and pull it along the surface of the ground. Another scout will crawl on his stomach and throw his rifle a few feet in front of him and repeat the process. Another will crawl forward with his rifle in the hollow of his elbows at right angles to his body.

STEALTH PATROL
OPENING TALK

It is never advisable to employ more than two men for this patrol. They must be highly trained in stalking and crawling and stealth, with much patience and pluck.

Functions.

To obtain prisoner or identification; to examine enemy defences; to cut wire; to locate machine guns or any other weapon likely to hold up the advance of our troops day or night; to locate enemy outposts and to listen for sounds from enemy talking or working.

Equipment.

Woollen caps or Balaclava style woollen headgear. Black face or cover with camouflage netting. From practical experience scouts prefer netting by day and blacking by night; under certain weather conditions at night the netting is inclined to impede vision. Gloves should be worn, preferably leather, woollen gloves are warm, but they are continually getting caught up in wire and brambles and are difficult to disentangle.

Unless otherwise ordered, no steel helmets should be worn and no respirator or web equipment. Ankle rubber boots (Canadian make) are excellent—light, warm, noiseless and waterproof—or canvas shoes; but these, worn at night over rough stony surfaces or rocks, are likely to cause injury to one's toes and feet; but if much water is to be encountered, canvas shoes are good as the water drains out through the canvas very quickly and there is no danger of the shoes making that squelching noise which occurs when rubber or leather boots get full of water. Long rubber boots should not be worn; they are inclined to make a " plop-plop " sort of noise which can be heard for some distance; if, however, it is imperative to wear " hip thigh " rubbers, then they should be turned down in a roll to reach half-way to the calf of the leg.

Leather jerkin. In cold, snow, mud and wintry weather, this type of coat can be worn inside out, and slits made in lining for pockets. Leather shines too much if worn in ordinary way.

No metal buttons or badges of course if they are polished, and no maps, letters or important documents.

Weapons.

Pistols : Holster carried on leather or narrow web belt in middle of back when crawling. If leather holster, it must not be polished leather.

Grenades : Two each. Most important in case of ambush or defence or attack.

Administrative.

No meal should be eaten immediately before going out. It is apt to induce sleep or feeling of sluggishness and flatulence, and is also inclined to make men cough if crawling on stomach. The last meal should be taken about three hours before patrol starts. Scouts should be given a hot meal on return and a drink of rum if obtainable.

METHOD

Practical demonstration to illustrate progressive training of the recruit as follows :—

Two trained scouts, correctly equipped, will advance in single file in an attempt to capture an enemy sentry who has been placed out in the open in front of onlookers, etc., so that all movements preparatory to and after capture can be plainly seen. The stealth patrol will advance a short distance crouching, then a few yards on hands and knees, and then, when about fifteen yards from sentry, the patrol will commence to crawl on their stomachs ; pistols in right hand, grenades in trouser pockets.

Attack.

When the leader considers he is in a suitable position for the final stealth rush, he will signal (arranged beforehand) to his partner to come up in line with him. This is important as when in line their movements can be synchronised to a second, whereas in file it is impossible for both men to work in unison. When the patrol is ready to strike it is usually arranged that the leader will transfer his pistol from his right hand to his left and with his right hand stealthily extract a grenade from his pocket. The leader will be responsible for guarding against an ambush or unexpected attack, and his partner will capture the sentry, using any particular method in which he has been trained. He will pass his hands *quickly* up and down the prisoner's body, feeling for knife or pistol, leader watching all round and keeping corner of eye on prisoner as well No time must be lost in getting prisoner away. Leader moves off at slow double, followed by prisoner (hands up) and with the second scout behind, pistol pointed at prisoner's back. Do not keep too close to prisoner—that is to say, the rear scout's pistol must not be touching prisoner, but about four feet away. Watch out for a cunning prisoner stopping suddenly and tripping the scout behind him and then dashing off into the darkness and making his escape. This concludes the demonstration.

STEALTH PATROL.

STEALTH PATROL.

Diagram.

Scouts starting out in single file, walking stooping ; then assume crouching position, followed by crawling on hands and knees, then crawling on stomach.   These positions are assumed in order to demonstrate the use of the individual movements as already displayed by the demonstration squad.

GETTING INTO LINE FOR THE FINAL STEALTH ASSAULT.

DEMONSTRATION TO ILLUSTRATE THE PROGRESSIVE TRAINING OF THE RECRUIT

THE DIAMOND FORMATION FOR RECONNAISSANCE PATROL

OPENING TALK

There are three main types of patrols. They are—

(i) The Fighting Patrol.
(ii) The Reconnaissance Patrol.
(iii) The Standing Patrol.

The Reconnaissance Patrol, using diamond formation, will now be demonstrated. It consists of four men only. This formation was adopted with much success during the Great War of 1914-1918 by scouts of the Canadian Army. Many British regiments also used this formation, including the Guards Division. It was used in this war by British patrols on the French front and in the Middle East.

Function.

The principal function is to obtain information—obtain this without unnecessary delay; to see without being seen; to guard against surprise; to regain and maintain touch with the enemy. Their function is not to fight unless absolutely necessary to obtain the information which is desired. This formation is excellent for all-round observation, and either for attack or defence.

Equipment.

The same as for Stealth Patrol.

Weapons.

The same as for Stealth Patrol. Some carry daggers or knives as well. If a knife is carried it should have a long blade (10 inches); short blade not of much value in hand-to-hand attack. In addition, each scout should carry two grenades.

Administrative.

The same as for Stealth Patrol.

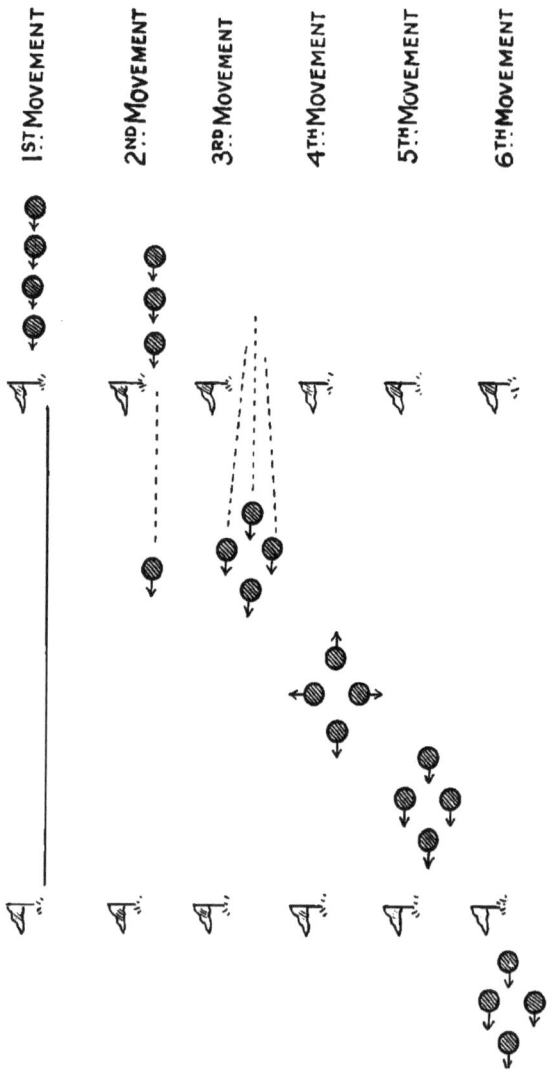

1ST MOVEMENT

2ND MOVEMENT

3RD MOVEMENT

4TH MOVEMENT

5TH MOVEMENT

6TH MOVEMENT

DIAGRAM 3.

54

METHOD

Practical demonstration as follows :—

To be carried out between two flags as per the diagram on opposite page.

A leader has been appointed who will lead the patrol in front ; also a second-in-command in case of leader becoming a casualty.

FIRST MOVEMENT.—The four scouts fall in behind one of the small flags (see diagram) in single file.

SECOND MOVEMENT.—The conducting officer points out that the patrol is now leaving its headquarters in the battle zone in order to regain touch with the enemy, or to follow any other important instructions received from the Company Commander or Battalion Commander. Due care must be observed from the start—an enemy patrol might be at the " front gate " on a similar mission to your own, so be careful—but at the same time remember that speed is essential and no time must be lost unnecessarily. Do not crawl without some very good reason—it is a very slow process.

It is night, not very dark—seeing distance, say, some twenty-five yards. The leader has arranged some simple signals with his patrol.

The leader's first job is to try to make sure that his patrol will not advance into an ambush, so that before his patrol clears its own protective headquarters the leader crawls out alone as far as he deems adequate and has ordered his patrol

to keep him in view. When he has gone far enough he will lie down and look and listen possibly for five minutes or so. His patrol will conform to his movements (see diagram).

THIRD MOVEMENT.—All is well. Leader signals for his patrol to join him and take up the diamond formation as practised. He signals by keeping his hand and arm close to the ground and waving them forward; they should proceed crawling on hands and knees—not necessary to crawl on

stomach. The men must all watch their leader and watch
their flanks as well. No. 4 man will be careful to look behind
him frequently. The scouts are now in diamond formation
and lying down. The heads of the two scouts on the flanks
should be in line with the leader's feet and at arm's length;
they should be able to touch his feet. No. 4 scout's head
should be in line with flankers, and he must be able to touch
their feet at arm's length.

FOURTH MOVEMENT.—After looking and listening, the leader
signals he is moving forward; he rises to his knees, and they
all crawl forward at a stealthy pace on hands and knees.

FIFTH MOVEMENT.—Suddenly but stealthily the leader sinks
to the ground on his stomach—it is supposed they are well
out in the battle zone; the scouts all conform to the movements
of their leader. He gives a quiet signal by tapping his heels
together. This denotes that the leader has, he thinks, heard
or seen something, and he requires all-round observation.

The scouts will now put into practice the turning round movement they have been taught.

When this movement has been completed, the conducting officer will remark : " That is the diamond formation. They have now all-round observation and hearing ; the leader has complete control (so difficult to maintain with large patrols) ; and if it is necessary to fight they can give a good account of themselves. They are lying flat on the ground and very difficult to see at a distance of a few yards."

SIXTH MOVEMENT.—At a signal from the leader they resume their former positions, rising to their hands and knees, moving forward for a few yards ; then rise stealthily to their feet and the demonstration is completed.

FINAL DEMONSTRATION

INDIVIDUAL STALK—SCOUT *v.* SCOUT

The conducting officer, if he has been giving his demonstration to a company or more of troops, will state that he will now conclude the work by putting on an individual stalk by two trained N.C.Os. If, on the other hand, the demonstration has been given by a Platoon Officer who is training his own recruits or men, then he should proceed as follows :—

Locate a piece of ground with reasonable amount of cover sufficient to hide a man when lying flat on the ground ; then divide his men into pairs. Place them from 50 yards to 80 yards apart. Then instruct them to lie down and on a signal move forward and stalk each other ; they must keep their heads down, look through cover or round cover, but not *over* cover ; must stop and listen frequently and try to locate sound ; also important to keep direction—watch for landmarks. The scout who spots his opponent first wins (holds up his hand). Possible to stalk to within a few feet of each other, without being seen. This is excellent practice.